A GIRL'S BEST FRIEND

A GIRL'S BEST FRIEND

Joanna Sandsmark

Images from the archives of
The Illustrated London News

RONNIE
SELLERS
PRODUCTIONS
PORTLAND, MAINE

For the Reuter women: Kay, Kitt, Beth, and Missy

First edition published in North America by
Ronnie Sellers Productions, Inc.
P.O. Box 818, Portland, Maine 04104
For ordering information:
(800) 625-3386 toll free
(207) 772-6814 fax
Visit our website: www.rsvp.com E-mail: rsp@rsvp.com

Ronnie Sellers: President and Publisher
Robin Haywood: Publishing Director
Mary Baldwin: Managing Editor

Images from the archives of The Illustrated London News Picture Library 2005
Text © Joanna Sandsmark 2005
Compilation © Carroll & Brown Limited 2005
All rights reserved.

ISBN: 1-56906-598-5

10 9 8 7 6 5 4 3 2 1

Reproduced by Colourscan, Singapore

Printed and bound in China by SNP Leefung

INTRODUCTION

They say that diamonds are a girl's best friend, and dogs are a man's best friend. I say balderdash! The truth is that dogs wearing diamonds are a girl's best friend.

Even without the trinkets, dogs are the lads who never let you down, the lasses who always support you, and the most loyal, trustworthy companions you will ever know. They love to cuddle, adore heavy petting, bring you gifts like sticks and dead things, and always look at you like you are the center of their universe. The sparkle in a dog's eyes matches the glisten in a diamond any day. Therefore, it's time to take back the title of "best friend" from the guys. Dogs are a girl's best friend!

What does your dog say about you?

Chances are you've chosen an animal that in some way complements your personality. Whether it's the sleek, elegant lines of a greyhound, the rambunctious playfulness of a cocker spaniel, or the high-energy work ethic of a Border collie, your dog is a reflection of some aspect of who you are inside. Emphasize this! Be proud of your choice of pet by showing the world that you are a woman who knows who she is, even if the answer is, "A mutt." After all, mutts combine the qualities of their doggie parentage, which simply means you're versatile and well rounded. And if you can't quite figure out your mutt's origins, be proud of your status as a woman of mystery.

There are some simple ways to make sure people don't see the wrong thing in your chosen companion. Always keep her well groomed – she'll be happier and so will you. Clean up after her, to prove you're both good neighbors. And always keep her on a leash. Tell her it's because you're such an attractive couple. She'll be sure to understand.

A dog is the only thing on this earth

that loves you

more than he loves himself.

JOSH BILLINGS

Treats

Just as it's important for you to treat yourself to a new pair of shoes, or the occasional getaway on a yacht with a handsome jewel thief, your dog also needs treats. Giving her something tasty will encourage certain behaviors and let you bond more closely.

A treat, however, will soon become a necessity in your dog's mind; the life span of something being an actual treat – i.e. special and unexpected – is anywhere from one to five incidents. After that, it becomes something so completely necessary for her existence that she will be willing to whine, pout, stare at you with big, longing eyes and, well, do the same things you did to get onto that yacht.

Indulge her. If she starts to pack on a little extra weight, walk her more often. Of course, after one to five extra walks that, too, will no longer be a treat, which means you will then be obligated to feed her more, walk her more, and accept that everything you're doing is now deemed a necessity. You really didn't expect to win the war of the treats, did you?

Corgi and Bess

You may find yourself attracted to a particular breed of dog above all others. Queen Elizabeth II has had a lifelong love affair with the Welsh corgi and the late Queen Mother was also a fan, as you can see in the photo on the right. Note the joyously serene expression on her face. When it comes to adoring a pet, emotion knows no status or station. We are all one in this, feeling only the deep and abiding bond between us and our beloved dogs.

Corgis have a rich history, embellished by legend. They're said to have been the creatures that pulled the coaches of the Fairy Queen, who, after such exemplary service, released them to the world at large. From one Queen to another, corgis have retained their appeal.

If you do find a breed that "speaks" to you above all others, listen to that voice. The various breeds don't just look dissimilar; they run the gamut of personalities. It's possible that your special breed is a gift of the fairies, just for you.

A dog, I will maintain, is a very tolerable judge of beauty, as appears from the fact that any liberally educated dog does, in a general way, prefer a woman to a man.

FRANCES THOMPSON

Why be friends?

Dogs have been with us for over 12,000 years and it's no wonder dogs and women get along so well – we both invest quite a bit of time training each other to be the perfect companion. You teach your dog to stay, sit, beg, and roll over. Your dog teaches you to scratch when his ears are itchy, walk with him when he feels the call of nature, and feed him when he's hungry. He spends countless hours instructing you which table scraps to drop his way, which people he will welcome to his home, where and how to stroke his fur in just the right way, the games he prefers with each toy, and which pieces of furniture are his to do with as he pleases.

When you think about how much time and energy your dog has invested in training you, it's a marvel he has the patience. Then again, your willingness to engage in his favorite behaviors is one of the primary reasons he worships you.

With today's hectic lifestyles, it's easy to forget how much your dog depends on you to make a little time for him. Instead of getting cranky when he asks for attention, or being so preoccupied that you barely notice him waiting patiently for you to see his need, take some time out of each day and make it all about him. Throw his favorite tennis ball, brush his coat, and talk to him in that special voice you use only for him. Your payment will be that happy doggie smile, a wagging tail, and maybe a big lick or two. Pretty good bargain, isn't it?

History's dog lovers

Hungarian Princess Vilma Lwoff-Parlaghy was so wild about her dogs that she nearly created an international incident. A prestigious hotel in New York City refused to allow pets, and the popular Princess took a "love me, love my dogs" attitude toward all of America. Happily, the situation was resolved when another prestigious hotel welcomed her, pets and all.

Empress Tz'u-hsi of China built a marble palace for her dogs.

Dorothy Leib Harrison Wood Eustis was one of the primary forces behind training guide dogs. She started a business in Switzerland breeding German Shepherds, switched from providing them for the police to training them for the blind, and then returned to her native United States to establish the seeing-eye movement in that country. She was so successful, and such an intelligent investor, that the seeing-eye organization is entirely self-sustaining.

Irene Castle, famous American dancer of the early 20th century, was a devoted dog owner. She started the Orphans of the Storm Animal Shelter, near Chicago, Illinois. Not too long before her death, she said, "When I die, my gravestone is to say 'humanitarian' instead of 'dancer.' I put it in my will. Dancing was fun, and I needed the money, but Orphans of the Storm comes from the heart. It's more important."

Queen Victoria was famous for her love of dogs. Her fascination even influenced the breeding of Pomeranians, which didn't gain popularity until the British monarch fell in love with the breed. In Sydney, Australia, the Queen Victoria Building boasts a statue of one of her dogs.

Conversations

Women, being verbal creatures, spend a lot of time talking to their dogs. If this sounds like you, you're on the right track. It's very important to share your voice with your furry friend. Dogs take some of their cues from nonverbal sources, but they are also very attuned to the human voice. Animals that live in a highly socialized culture, like the pack animals that gave us the modern dog, tend to be far more verbal than their solitary brethren.

Your dog wants nothing more than to feel loved and included in your family. So talk to him! Tell him what you did that day, how you feel, and that you love him. Look him in the eyes and speak in the voice that makes you sound a bit like an idiot but it gets him so darn happy and tail-waggy you exaggerate it even more.

Don't forget to use his name when you're having this loving conversation. You don't want him to associate his name only with discipline and "bad dog!" commands. Help him to love his name by using it as often as possible during your sweet talk.

Dogs make excellent protectors,

except when they're puppies.

Puppies will draw strangers to you

more efficiently than if you were

handing out money.

ANONYMOUS

Cute can be better than beautiful

Age may bring gravitas but gravity is not always our friend. Sure, it keeps our feet on the ground, but it's forever trying to pull the rest of us down to join them. Instead of frowning at that fold of skin around your middle, the gray in your hair or that new set of jowls, remember they can be quite adorable.

The pug, a dog that originated in China, is renowned for his folds of skin. Pugs were often the choice of royalty and they still retain that air of dignity. Even if they're clowning around, they do it with poise and élan.

The Cesky terrier has a luxurious coat that can range from blue-gray to dark slate-gray. With its silky luster, it makes it impossible not to pet. Lovable, family-oriented, and great with kids, the Cesky never feels shame at being gray-haired, so why should you?

As for those jowls of yours, they're nothing compared to the bulldog! This tenacious but loveable dog has enough jowl action to outdo any of his human counterparts. So stop fretting about the signs of aging and instead, be kind to your inner dog. After all, cute is cute, and that includes you.

Exercise

Walking the dog is one of the necessities of ownership. But how you do it is up to you. Sure, you can plod along, looking bored and grumpy, wishing your dog's call of nature would just be quiet. Or you can make it an event.

If you have a dog park nearby, you could find several opportunities to meet handsome gentlemen who share your love for pets. Make sure you look casually stunning, and choose a man whose dog is a compatible breed with your own.

In the city, you can sashay down the street, high heels clicking, hips swaying, and dog relieving himself. Try to time this so that you aren't scooping up something unmentionable when Mr. Right walks past.

The benefits for you and your dog are immeasurable. You'll get lots of fresh air and exercise, which aids both your figure and your health, and you could meet some very interesting people along the way. It also helps to keep your house free from accidents for that time when you bring home a handsome stray or two.

Famous dogs in cinema

Rin Tin Tin was Hollywood's first major canine star. Born in Germany and brought to the United States after World War I, he made 25 films. He became his studio's highest wage earner, and even signed his own contracts with a paw print!

One of the most famous screen dogs was Lassie. She was played by a male collie named "Pal." Pal got the role because he was able to do a whitewater stunt when the original female collie chosen for the role would have nothing to do with it. The collie's white blaze down the nose had been seen as undesirable and was almost bred out of the species. When Lassie became a star, everyone wanted a dog like "her," and that included the blaze.

The Walt Disney Studio has had several successes using dogs in central roles. Their most famous dog films were both animated: "The Lady and the Tramp" (1955) and "101 Dalmatians" (1961). The standout scene in the former comes when the two leads share a plate of spaghetti. In the latter, the evil Cruella DeVille is one of the most memorable screen villains in history when she decides to make a coat out of the Dalmatian puppies.

If you are a dog and your owner

suggests that you wear a sweater ...

suggest that [she]

wear a tail.

FRAN LEBOWITZ

For appearance's sake

Women and their dogs share a bond that goes very deep. Throughout the ages, both have been shaped and, in some ways, tortured, to make themselves more appealing.

Women have had to put up with corsets, girdles, whalebone stays, and underwire bras, all in an effort to appear more "perfect" to men. Dogs have gone through countless cycles of breeding, having traits chosen that give a visual appeal, but may be detrimental to the dog's health.

Boxers, for example, are bred for short snouts and that can lead to lifelong respiratory problems. Women had their own source of respiratory problems when they used to wear corsets with whalebone stays. (It didn't do the whales much good, either.) Some corsets were so constricting

that women could barely breathe and had to refrain from all physical activity. Even the girdles that took over from corsets were often painful and constricting. Then again, it's easier to buy a girdle than to give up chocolate.

Chinese foot binding resulted in a lifetime of pain and very limited mobility, all in an effort to look attractive. Some of today's stiletto heels might be seen in a similar light. However, they do make your calves look really good.

Unconditional love

There are few, if any, relationships in a woman's life that can equal the unconditional love you'll get from your pet. You are the center of his life, and when he looks at you, he is gazing into the eyes of his own personal goddess.

He would willingly give his life for yours. He would walk to the ends of the Earth to be with you. He will wait patiently all day, just for whatever moments you choose to give him. And in return, you feed him, play with him, groom him, walk him, and gaze into his eyes with all the love in your heart. The bond you share cannot be broken. He may get into trouble or test your patience, but always there is a deep feeling of belonging together.

When you're sad or lonely, he magically appears by your side, wanting to comfort you with his unguarded spirit. When you're happy or excited, he shares your enthusiasm, wagging his tail, barking his agreement, and maybe punctuating the moment with a leap or a lick on your face.

You'll never have a more loyal, loving friend than your dog. And for him, it is the answer to his prayers to have a goddess as loving as you are.

My goal in life is
to be as good a person as
my dog already thinks I am.

UNKNOWN

Etiquette

Your idea of proper social etiquette may differ from that of your dog. When attending a garden party, you probably wouldn't lie on your back with your limbs in the air, begging someone to rub your belly. And most likely, you would eschew greeting male guests by sniffing their trousers. Note: if you do usually introduce yourself in these ways, then dog etiquette is the least of your problems.

Don't punish your dog for being a dog. Instead, pretend you taught her these behaviors. This will make your dog appear obedient, and you'll be applauded for being an excellent trainer. A cheeky command, like "Find the drugs!" when she heads for someone's trousers, will also help solidify your reputation.

Smaller dogs have an advantage in social situations, being less visually intrusive. A miniature Yorkie on your lap with legs casually pawing the air is usually perceived as cute and irresistible. However, if you sit with a Great Dane on your lap, the sight of his enormous splayed legs will most likely cause undue attention. Use common sense, and remember – whatever she's doing, you taught her that.

Dog tales

Angie and Mickey

Like many expectant mothers, Angie would often wake up at night, hungry. Her husband was out of the country for several months, so she was alone with her little black Chihuahua, Mickey. After a few nights of watching Angie get up to eat something, Mickey knew what he had to do. When Angie joined him on the bed, he would jump off and fetch a doggie snack. He would put the snack by her shoulder, push it under her pillow with his nose, and then return to his blanket, satisfied that he had taken care of Angie, as was his duty.

Missy, Harley, and Hooties

Missy loved her canine family. But as Harley, a Welsh terrier, and Hooties, a wire haired fox terrier, aged, health problems set in for both of them. When Missy and her husband moved into their new home on six wooded acres, it seemed like the perfect place for the two terriers to live out the rest of their lives.

Unfortunately, both dogs, now blind and deaf, were frightened of the new place, and were unable to navigate it without injury. Missy made the difficult decision to put them both down together. On her way to the vet, Missy took the dogs to their former home, opened the back gate and let them spend their last hours on Earth in a place that was familiar and beloved.

Pam and Sugar

Teenaged Pam loved her white terrier mix, Sugar. One day, Pam smart-mouthed her mother and got a pretty good spanking from her father. Afterwards, Sugar cuddled with Pam for hours, trying to make her feel better, until the dog finally had to go outside. Sugar marched out of the room, past Pam's dad without looking at him, and went to the back door. She snubbed him again when she returned. He couldn't even tempt her with a treat. In fact, Sugar refused to have anything to do with him for a full week. That's telling him, Sugar!

Three is never a crowd

If your spouse is worried that a canine addition to the family will take all of your attention, reassure him that although true, you'll still remember him when it's time to lift large bags of dog food, during torrential rain, or when it's time to see the vet.

Many young couples who aren't quite ready for children, adopt a puppy as a trial run. They experience what it's like to share attention, to be responsible for another being's welfare, and even how to steal a few "alone time" moments when the dog relinquishes the bed. It's a great training ground for the enormous responsibility that'll come when you forget to take your pill.

These couples learn that, contrary to their conviction that $1 + 1 =$ happiness, three is never a crowd when the newest member of the family walks on four legs. Instead of resenting the puppy's presence, they learn the joy of spoiling their beloved new family member and delighting in her every step toward adulthood. They learn how to discipline, and how to forgive. They learn how to put themselves second when another's need is greater. In essence, they learn what it's like to be a family.

In praise of small dogs

Terriers, Chihuahuas, dachshunds, corgis, Pekinese, pugs, and miniatures of all types may have different personalities, coats, and temperaments, but all can fit on your lap.

Oh, the joy of snuggling with that little, warm body. Petting her on the belly. Getting a big lick on the face. Gazing into those adoring eyes as they look up at you from the haven of your arms. That's the blessing of a small dog.

It's adorable to watch their energetic antics, and hear the bravado in their yipping barks. Small dogs never see themselves as small. In their minds, they are every bit as fierce as their larger counterparts. They're dogs, and that means something, regardless of size.

If you have a small dog, sing her praises! Enjoy the closeness and the companionship. Bring her with you, if pets are allowed. She'll keep you company and won't take up much room. Wherever your dog goes, she is the guardian of the heart of your family. A big job for a small frame, but as she would eagerly tell you, she's always up to the challenge.

[Dogs] are better than human beings,
because they know but do not tell.

EMILY DICKiNSON

The racing dog

Dog racing is called "The Sport of Queens." The history books will say it's because Queen Elizabeth I started the first dog racing track. In reality, it's because race day means you get to act like a queen. First, you have the excuse to wear large hats. Large hats have sadly gone out of vogue for most activities, but a day in the sun allows women the excuse of large hat-wearing.

Once you are at the track in your large hat, let the men ogle and worship you. Pretend to be there for the dogs, but in reality, what you need is a stake. After enough ogling some man is going to offer to place a bet for you. This is when things get interesting.

How do you choose which dog to bet on? Some will tell you to study the field, ground conditions, trainers, past records, and all those other tedious statistics. It's far more fun to bet based on the dog's name. Imagine winning simply because the dog bore the same initials as your cousin's best friend from school? You'll be seen as a genius. And if he's a long shot, you'll be a wealthy genius in a large hat.

You wear him well

There is a trend with the new breed of hip, young celebrities to accessorize their haute couture by carrying a dog. Paris Hilton is rarely seen without Tinkerbell, her pet Chihuahua. When in public, both Paris and Tinkerbell are usually wearing the latest fashions. Have dogs become the new jewelry?

One does have to wonder if celebrities take care of their dogs like the simple folk do. In Hollywood, if a service is possible, there is someone out there who will do it. There are professional dog walkers, who make sure that Fifi gets her exercise so that Mommy can work out with her personal trainer. And there are groomers who pay house calls. It wouldn't do for a movie star to mingle with the common folk.

However, there are also stars who are very involved in their dogs' lives. Halle Berry takes her two toy Maltese with her everywhere. Denise Richards proved her loyalty while making

a film in England. Because of the quarantine laws, she had to leave her four dogs at home while she worked. Unwilling to be separated for so long a time, she flew home every weekend, just to spend some quality time with the pooches.

So are dogs just accessories to a celebrity, or are they far more? As with all things, it isn't about shoving people into a group and expecting them all to act the same. Celebrities are just as individual as the rest of us, and therefore they each treat their dogs in their own way.

Your dog, your child

Don't ever let anyone try to convince you that your dog is not your child. She's your baby. You feed her, teach her, clean up after her, love her – the same things you do with any child (or husband, actually, but that's a different story). Anyone who tries to convince you otherwise has simply never fallen in love with a dog.

Because she is your baby, it's important to take lots of photographs of her, brag about her to your friends, and indulge her every whim. When she does things right, praise and encourage her. It's important to build up her self-esteem. If she misbehaves, be firm, but loving. Never strike her. Physical violence has no place in a happy household.

If you need to stay away for extended periods, be sure you have a trustworthy sitter or dog nanny. The life of your darling is in this person's hands. Don't leave her with Great Aunt Olga who cannot stand dogs, even if she does work cheap. Finally, lavish your beloved with attention. She needs your affection more than anything else in the world. If you do this, she will reward you with loyalty, devotion, obedience, and the special gift of her entire doggie heart.

If you think dogs can't count,
try putting three dog biscuits in your
pocket and then giving Fido
only two of them.

PHIL PASTORET

Pitfalls of dog ownership

1 Your dog is probably cuter than you.

2 The posh condo you dream about doesn't allow pets.

3 Vet fees are so high that if you pass within 30 yards of a veterinary clinic, they send you a bill.

4 When things get intimate between you and your significant other, your dog takes up half the bed.

5 Your expensive silk blouse is so covered in dog hair that your date thought it was a sweater.

6 Finding that little "message" on the carpet ... in your bare feet.

7 Bringing home a date who is clever, handsome, wealthy, and perfect – then finding out he doesn't like dogs. You have to kick him out, the louse.

8 Going hungry when dining out so you can take home most of your meal in a doggie bag (Pepper does love a good filet mignon).

9 Stinting on your own personal grooming so you can keep your pet looking her best.

10 Owning lots of things with chew marks.

Big is beautiful

Great Danes, St. Bernards, rottweilers, German shepherds, Labradors, Irish wolfhounds, and mastiffs are all wonderful dogs who are big, big, and bigger! Though large, big dogs can fit easily into any woman's heart.

Big dogs make great protectors. Even if they aren't aggressive, their sheer size will intimidate most would-be attackers. With deep-throated barks, they may bother the neighbors, but if you have room to run, then a big dog could be your perfect pet.

There's nothing quite like the feeling of hugging a large dog around the neck, knowing that the two of you share a unique bond. A rub on the belly, a quick game of fetch, or a rambling walk in the park cements the relationship between you and your friendly giant.

Watching an ungainly puppy with huge paws and a head too big for its body grow into a delightful presence that cannot be ignored, is a thrill only a big dog lover will truly understand. Having all that power hanging on your every word, patiently waiting for your attention makes you feel just a little bigger yourself.

Heroic Dogs

Police dogs

Dogs have a variety of law enforcement duties in today's world. There are tracking dogs that can hunt down a fleeing suspect or follow a scent trail from the scene of the crime back to the perpetrator's origin. There are drug-sniffing dogs that can locate hidden, illegal drugs that no human could. There are also explosive-sniffing dogs who are helping to keep us safe in these uncertain times. Cadaver dogs can find the remains of a murder victim in a seemingly hopeless tangle of nature. Police dogs are specially trained, and often work with a single officer. The dog's loyalty to that officer is as close and trustworthy as the relationship between any officer and his or her partner.

Fire dogs

It's not just the familiar follower of fire trucks, the Dalmatian, that is associated with firefighters anymore. Arson dogs are trained to find traces of accelerants in the remains of fires that are suspicious. The sensitivity of a dog's nose is so great that he can detect the scent in something as small as a thousandth of a drop.

Rescue dogs

When the World Trade Center towers fell on September 11, 2001, rescue dogs became the primary tool in the search for survivors. Rescue dogs are often sent to the scenes of disasters, both natural and man-made. Whether it's a St. Bernard in an avalanche, or a highly trained German shepherd pawing at debris, the heroism of a rescue dog is never questioned.

Guide dogs

Giving the blind protection, self-esteem, and independence in a sighted world, guide dogs are the epitome of a working, heroic dog. Specially trained German shepherds, Labrador retrievers and golden retrievers make up the bulk of the guide canines. Guide dogs can help a blind person cross a busy street, navigate through a teeming market, and wend their way through a crowded restaurant. They'll go anywhere their master wants to go. That's independence.

Training your dog

It's important to train your dog. Not that you have to train her to ride a tricycle, jump through fire hoops, or chase criminals. But basic behaviors like house training, teaching her to sit or heel, and letting her know which furniture is off limits, are important social skills.

Men and women have different approaches to dog training, as they do in life. The trick is to take advantage of those areas where women are often better than men. Patience, for example, is an attribute many women share, and it's an essential ingredient in good dog training.

When you teach a new behavior, be consistent, be patient, and take things one step at a time. Remember to be firm — you are the leader of the pack, and the dog must be aware of this. But firm does not mean violent or cruel. Take your ego out of the mixture, and focus your training time purely on your pet. Lead her toward the new behavior with kindness, never losing your temper, or showing too much disappointment. Eventually, you will succeed. Life can be better for you and for your dog when you work together to achieve your goals.

The sporting dog

Sure, walking the dog is good exercise, and gets the job done for the dog, but there are so many other ways women can spend quality active time with their pets.

With a big dog, a good harness (a regular leash won't work, as the dog needs to pull you), safety equipment for you, and a pair of inline skates, you and Fido can enjoy some quality time at the park or beach. Before attempting this activity, you should already be a good inline skater. Being pulled by a dog when you have no control over your own feet isn't a bright idea. If it's winter, try it on ice skates. Or just let him slip alongside you on a frozen lake or pond.

If you like hunting, and you might be surprised how many women do, then you probably know all about the joys of a good retriever, flusher, or pointer. If hunting isn't your style, then you might enjoy taking your dog for a swim. Many breeds adore the water, and will doggie paddle right alongside you as you enjoy cooling off on a hot summer day.

The new single mother

With more and more women joining the workforce and focusing on their careers, the traditional roles of women as wives and mothers are fading. A high-powered, well-paid career can be very satisfying. It can also leave little time for dating or thoughts of marriage. Where is this new generation of independent, career-oriented females getting the love, affection, and attention everyone craves? From their dogs.

The modern, unmarried, over 30 woman is the fastest-growing segment of dog-owners, and it hasn't gone unnoticed. Shops are springing up all over that cater to these young, financially independent dog owners. With pooch in tow, they buy treats and trinkets, books and clothing, fancy dog collars and gourmet chewies. With no husbands or children to spoil, their loving attention falls squarely on their pet. Their dog becomes their child, something many pet owners can understand.

So why not spoil little Fluffy, as long as you can afford it? Thus far, not a single dog has complained about the extra attention.

The disposition of noble dogs is
to be gentle with people they know
and the opposite with those
they don't know ...
How, then, can the dog be anything other
than a lover of learning since it defines
what's its own and what's alien.

PLATO

Stage dogs

Dog acts have been around for as long as there have been stages on which to present them. The athleticism and grace of dogs make them naturals for circuses, vaudeville, and magic acts.

In 1901, Thomas Edison produced a short film called "Miss Laura Comstock's Bag Punching Dog." The film begins with a well-dressed Laura and her boxer "Mannie" staring at the camera. It cuts to a stage where Mannie stands alone, looking like he has better things to do. A large punching bag descends from above and Mannie attacks. With each "punch" the bag swings wildly and Mannie leaps, twists, and twirls in the air to give yet another blow. Eventually he catches the ball and shakes it in his mouth like a fresh kill.

In the United Kingdom, stage shows were filled with performing dog acts, many trained and presented by women, until the 1920s, when Dog's Trust (NCDL) succeeded in getting them outlawed.

Performing dogs haven't disappeared, however. Even today, there are women with acrobatic dog acts touring in many places around the globe. There's just

something irresistible about watching dogs leap and twist, walk on their hind legs, and defy gravity on a tightrope.

Amazing dog stories

❖ In Nairobi, Kenya, a stray dog found an abandoned baby in a forest, picked him up gently in her mouth, ran across a busy road, through some barbed wire, and placed him in her litter of puppies, where he was later found and rescued.

❖ A woman was making some formula for her baby when the dog raced into the kitchen and started barking wildly. She tried to let him out, but he'd have none of it, going from the kitchen to the hallway, and continuing to bark and whine. Finally, she followed him into the baby's room and saw that the child was gasping for air and turning blue. At the hospital, the parents were told that the baby had double pneumonia and would have died if they hadn't discovered her exactly when they did. Ironically, the dog that saved the baby's life had almost lost his own a year earlier when a tumor was found in his liver. Although an operation put a financial strain on the family, the woman had refused to consider anything else. If she hadn't saved him, he wouldn't have been there to save the baby.

❖ In a psychiatric home in Frankfurt, Germany, a patient locked herself in the bathroom and placed a knife at her throat. She was determined to commit suicide until the police, learning that she was a dog lover, brought a small mixed breed pup to the scene. Upon seeing him pushing his mug into a crack in the door, the woman dropped the knife and gathered the dog in her arms. He was later given an award (a bone) by the government for stopping a suicide.

❖ A 12-year-old girl got separated from her family on an outing and wandered into an isolated ravine. Another family's dog followed her and stayed with her for 24 hours while searchers hunted for her. She survived the below-freezing temperatures at night because the dog barked nonstop, keeping her awake. When they were finally rescued, the girl was cold and hungry but otherwise healthy, thanks to the stalwart canine.

Why do women love dogs?

In June 2004, Newspoll conducted a survey of 242 dog-owning Australian women, aged 25 and older. Over 90 percent of those surveyed said they enjoyed the unconditional love and companionship a dog can provide. Although it might make you wonder what the other 10 percent were thinking, at least it proves that nine out of 10 dog-owning women recognized the canine's greatest attribute. There is no substitute for the adoration of your four-legged friend.

Sixty percent of the women said that dogs were more affectionate than men. Keep that in mind when you say, "Men are dogs" — it may not be your intention to bestow so high a compliment. Seventy-five percent turned to their dogs for affection when they felt down. What better support is there than a warm heart that won't argue with you, won't blame you, won't judge you, but will be there instantly when needed?

Nine out of 10 enjoyed petting their dog, and 88 percent admitted to spoiling him with treats and presents. Seventy-one percent described their dog as their friend. To my mind, that number should be 100 percent.

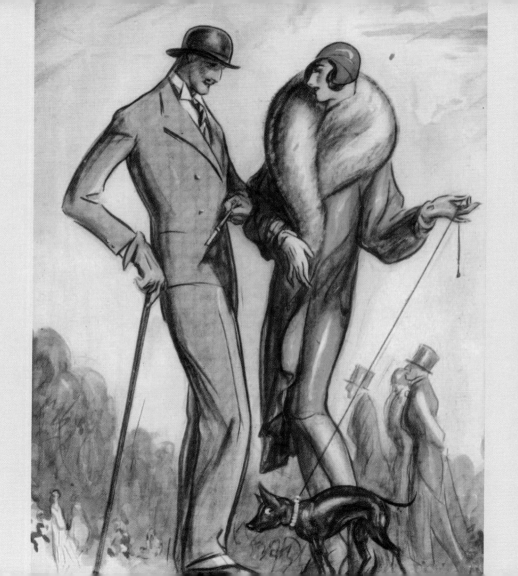

If a dog will not come to you after having
looked you in the face, you should go
home and examine your conscience.

WOODROW WILSON

The perfect mate

During the Renaissance, men kept large dogs to help them with their hunting. Women, however, found themselves attracted to small dog breeds. Miniaturized terriers and spaniels were especially popular. The men of the day weren't too keen about the women's interest in these pets. In fact, the very first man to write about dogs, Johannes Caius, claimed that dogs had no purpose. He despised the fact that women would allow the dogs to sit on their laps and lick their faces. He found the behavior lewd and "wanton."

Things didn't get better after that. Men continued to rail against women who kept dogs as pets; they found the closeness between a woman and her dog to be "unnatural." Physicians would advise men to kill pet dogs. Women, they postulated, would have no interest in bearing children as long as they had such a loving pet.

Eventually, men figured out that what they thought really didn't matter. If a woman wanted a dog, she was going to get one. And if his dream lady has such a companion, then a man had better treat her dog well, or she would never forgive him. Finally, some sanity!

Love me, love my dog

The semi-nomadic Gond people of central India have an unusual custom when it comes to dogs. They clear land by using the slash-and-burn method, but this puts them in the path of many wild animals. Some of these encounters are fatal. When a woman's husband is killed, especially by a tiger, she will often remarry. Nothing too strange about that, except that she marries a dog.

The Gond believe that dead husbands immediately inhabit whatever animal killed them. Because of this, if a widow were to marry again, the tiger with the first husband's spirit would kill the second husband. So, in an effort to fool the first husband's spirit, the widow marries the dog. This way, the late husband will kill the dog, and the widow is then free to marry another man.

Although your dog may give you more affection and loyalty than your husband, the Gond tradition is probably not something you should consider. It's too rough on the pooch. It's much easier to instruct your husband to avoid tigers. You can tell him that you're simply looking out for the welfare of the family pet. Oh, and him, too.

The more I see of men

the more I like dogs.

MADAME de STAEL

Dog shows

From humble beginnings, dog shows have become big business across the globe. It takes a special dog, and a special owner, to compete in the high stakes world of the international dog shows. Best of Breed, Best in Show – these are terms that yesterday's pet owner may not have heard. But now dog shows are getting in-depth television coverage, and all sorts of publicity. There was even a film spoofing the world of show dogs called "Best In Show" (2000).

If you are considering entering your dog in a show, there is one very important thing to keep in mind: you are also going to be judged. Get Fifi her fluffiest, train her how to walk in front of crowds, and do as much as you can to get her to win, but then take the time to worry about yourself. Make sure you can strut effortlessly in stiletto heels when holding onto her leash. Dress professionally, but sexy enough to capture the eye of the male judges. Learn some tricks: it's important to be able to smile without wrinkling, jog without too much bouncing, and always – always – be sure the camera gets your best side. Only then will you, er, your dog, have a chance at winning!

Bonding

Many women find they have a strong and lasting bond with their pet. With some, it's a little too strong. If you start looking like your dog, you may want to do a quick review as to whether you are identifying a little too heartily with your pooch.

It is not necessary for you to mimic your dog's look by cutting and dying your hair to match hers. Sure, it's cute for a photo op, but you'll get strange looks at the market when you walk in with hair that resembles two floppy ears. If you can't help your urge to become Rover's twin, choose the breed carefully. It's better to strive for the elegant lines of a greyhound or the haute couture of a poodle, than to lust after the heavy jowls of a bulldog or the wrinkled mug of a shar-pei.

It's also important to keep in mind that what looks natural on your dog may not translate so well to you. For example, even if you're dressed to the nines and have perfect makeup, excessive drooling and guttural growls are going to ruin the effect. It also makes it difficult to get a decent table at a restaurant.

Medium isn't rare

Cocker spaniels, bulldogs, beagles, and bull terriers can all be found in that wonderful in-between group, the medium dog. Perfect as family pets, they aren't so large as to cause problems by overwhelming or frightening children, and yet they aren't so small that they can be harmed underfoot by a rambunctious brood.

Medium dogs fit into nearly every environment: a home with children, an apartment, or running through your acreage. While of a manageable size if you need to take them to the vet, they are big enough to hold their own with many neighborhood dogs. Their appetites are moderate, their energy is high enough to have fun, and their affection is always welcome without being overwhelming.

Medium dogs come in a variety of shapes, temperaments, colors, breeds, and mixtures. The cocker spaniel is filled with playful joy, the beagle exudes friendly energy, the bulldog has a gentle calm, and the Manchester terrier is affectionate and intelligent. If you can't decide between big or small, then you should really consider one of the wonderful medium dogs. In the dog world, there's nothing average about being medium!

When you leave them in the morning,

they stick their nose in the door crack

and stand there like a portrait

until you turn the key eight hours later.

ERMA BOMBECK

No bad dogs, only bad owners

If your dog has bad habits, like jumping on visitors, wolfing down his food, or going on extended shopping sprees, look to yourself and what you've been teaching your dog. Do you jump on visitors out of a need for physical closeness? Do you attack your refrigerator late at night and scarf down entire containers of ice cream in a fit of emotional self-medicating? Do you keep your credit cards in the open where your dog can get at them? Remember, he watches you and learns what is right and wrong through your guidance.

Don't allow your dog to become a nuisance. If you talk on the phone for eight hours solid, why wouldn't he bark throughout the night? If you spend hours preening in front of a mirror, why wouldn't he lick his privates in the middle of a dinner party? So be kind to your dog by setting a good example.

When he does behave well, reward him as you would wish to be rewarded. Buy him a bejeweled collar, treat him to a steak dinner, or give him some "me" time where he is the center of attention. With enough rewards, the strains of "good dog" will soon be joined by "good owner."

Idioms and expressions

Hair of the dog that bit you Today, this means drinking alcohol to cure a hangover. The origin of the expression comes from the 1600s. Rabid dogs roamed the streets and a bite was certain death. But if you could grab a hair from the dog's coat and place it on your wound, you would be instantly cured.

Raining cats and dogs This expression means heavy rains. One theory to its origin is that in Medieval times dogs and cats used to sleep on thatched roofs at night. When it rained the roofs became slippery, and the dogs and cats would "rain" down from above.

Dog days The extremely hot days of mid- to late-summer are so named because of the dog star "Sirius." It's in the same part of the sky as the sun.

Straw dogs When you present an inferior idea, hoping that the listener will choose the better idea to follow, the former is a straw dog. "Heaven and Earth are not humane. They regard all things as straw dogs," wrote Lao-Tzu, an ancient Chinese philosopher. In early China, dog tokens made of straw were sacrificed and discarded – a pretty clear indication that straw dog ideas tend not to have much staying power.

Dog eat dog The original expression came from a Roman named Marcus Tarentius Varro, who said, "Dog does not eat dog," meaning everything has its limits. But by the 16th century, things had become more cut-throat, and the expression was changed to "Dog eat dog," showing that many thought there were no limits to man's competitive nature.

Dog in the manger Why was the dog in the manger? It wasn't there to eat the hay, but rather to keep any other animals from doing so. That's why this expression means spiteful and mean-spirited.

Three-dog night In northern climes, especially those whose cultures used sled dogs, a measure of how cold it was at night was determined by the number of dogs you needed in your tent to keep you warm. A three-dog night is very cold indeed.

acknowledgments

All images are from The Illustrated London News Picture Library, including

p.30 Yevonde Portrait Archive/ILN Picture Library
p.54 David Wright/ILN Picture Library

PICTURE LIBRARY

All images in this book are available to order as prints from www.ilnprints.co.uk

Author's Acknowledgment: My gratitude to the following women for sharing their

stories with me: Agneta Probst, Allison Felstein, Pam Payne, Emalou

Sandsmark, Kitt Reuter-Foss, and Shawn Keehne.